M. G. ALEXANDER

Success Unleashed

12 proven strategies to bring abundance into your work and life

This book was professionally typeset on Reedsy.
Find out more at reedsy.com

Contents

1

Introduction

Building a career is hard work. It takes a literal lifetime. Many of us work so hard and look up one day to a paltry bounty. All the hard work, all the missed events, all the late nights. In the end, all we have to show for it is (hopefully) a 401(k), maybe an IRA, maybe a home and a little money on the side. We all live according to our means and the absolute dollar value in those accounts barely matters. It just does not feel like enough for a lifetime of dedicated work. Add daily news about mass layoffs keeping most of us employees locked into jobs and careers we tolerate at best, despise at worst. We stop seeking fulfillment and icing to the illusion of safety our current jobs provide. In this context, social media and influencers coined the term "quiet quitting" and I am the first to empathize. Why even try, when you could lose it all at the whim of a financial manager declaring it so. The picture is bleak.

This is why I wrote this book. I wrote this book because I wanted to share my experience with building a career as a millennial. I believe I've carved out a successful professional career for myself using easy to replicate strategies and hacks. They did not only lead to a better work environment, more fulfillment and more money and promotions. They also provided a better balance in my life. I started worrying less about work and adjusting my life goals. Since I joined the workforce a decade and a half ago, my generation has been described as lazy, entitled and difficult to manage. I've been to hundreds of "working with/selling to/managing millennials" seminars and presentations. The only thing they have in common: they are WRONG. While most media blame the current professional environment, it is my strong belief that there are simple mechanisms for anyone, even a millennial or a Gen Zer, to be successful at work and life. We all can embrace the failures of the modern workplace while creating a life for ourselves that is a success.

In this book I will go through 12 methods I've tested personally and witnessed thousands of people use to unlock their success and begin to truly enjoy their careers and lives. Some of these strategies are straightforward, others require a little more work. I do not claim to have THE ANSWER. In most cases, I do suggest a twist to a more traditional approach and I'd recommend the reader pay attention to the subtleties. In other cases, I believe I've discovered for myself legitimate hacks that have enabled me to sail through situations where others struggle heavily. Any reader can pick up any of these strategies and adapt and adopt them into their lives. They may not fit perfectly and some fine tuning may be required, but the effects will be noticeable.

At this stage, I'd also like to remind the reader that actions compound and doing something once may not yield much results, but doing it over and over will eventually lead to massive results. Do not be discouraged and keep working at this to unleash the success you deserve!

2

Why Me?

Before we go into the strategies, some readers may be wondering why they should read my point of view. What makes me uniquely positioned to share this? What special gift was given to me that I would be an authority on the subject?

The answer is simple: I am not special. I did not have connections in the world of business and money. I did not have a particular mentor coaching me. I went to school, went to college, got my degree. Then I went to work and thought that hard work would give me all I wanted. I am just like you. My path was not destined to be great. Growing up middle class and focusing on school, going to college and getting an average job in a large corporation. I started out as a number on a page for the CEO of the company and probably for several people below him. I had no connections that made me special. And yet, by my measure - which is the only one that matters - I succeeded.

In a 15 year span after graduating college, I received numerous promotions, largely ahead of everyone else with my experience. I moved across countries and continents by choice. I made time for my personal life and found the love of my life. I've traveled all over and experienced a full life, all while earning a great living and being able to choose for myself. My physical fitness kept improving well into my thirties and I even carved out time for mental health. When I got bored, it was my decision to move to the next stage of my career and life. I had as much control over my next steps as one can have in a corporate setting.

It is these lessons that I am sharing here. While they may not be the recipe for success, they are the ingredients. Learn them, try them, adapt them and you'll be looking at a life that is built to your needs, preferences and lifestyle. No one else can dictate what your life looks like when you are being successful.

3

What Is Success?

On my first day in a full time job in my life, I thought "I'm going to be the CEO of the company". I know not everyone thinks that way, but everyone would agree that becoming the CEO of a ten thousand plus employee company is success. We are raised in an environment that is hyper competitive. It seems that success means climbing the corporate ladder or making a ton of money as an independent artist or sportsperson. While in the recent past, Gen Z may have redefined that a little with the whole influencer scene, ultimately, for most of us at the bottom of the ladder in any job, it seemed that it would take X promotions to "make it". I started on that path and everyone around me cheered me on.

As a decently smart guy, I did as good a job with my minimal responsibilities as I could. The idea was that through hard work and attention to detail, I would be able to impress my boss. He would then promote me and whenever his time to move on was here, I would get his job. Pretty straightforward, right? The people around me looked less ambitious and I could clearly identify their flaws. I thought I knew how I would beat them for my boss' job. I was scheming. And successfully too! My plan was in place and in five years' time I'd have his job. Five years later, I'd have his boss' job and after that it would only take another 5-10 years to become the company CEO.

And to my surprise: it was working. I actually got promoted among the quickest in my "class". After 2 years on the job, I thought I had this success thing figured out. *I don't need all those self-help books on how to succeed in your career. I am soaring and no one will catch me.* The next promotion soon followed and although I had made a lateral move in between, I was completely on pace to achieve my original boss' level by year 5. The stars were lining up.

Then came the twist - my boss who was due to retire soon was pushed out early and the job was split in two and reassigned to other existing managers. My "easy" step up had disappeared in the name of efficiency and cost savings. The rug was pulled from under my feet. It felt awful. The embarrassment was real. It felt real. And yet, in hindsight, no one knew that this was my goal. That this was my certain path to success. All anyone saw was a mid-20s kid, already in a more senior role than most of his peers who suddenly had a new boss. From that point on, by all external measures, I stagnated. I was not a failure, but it was a far cry from being a success.

And yet, I would claim that the following 5 years were the most successful in my life. Although I don't advocate comparing yourself to anyone, I'd claim I was one of the most successful people I knew.

The key to that success? Defining it for yourself. External measures mean nothing. Titles mean nothing. Even money means nothing. It is all made up. The *only thing* that matters is what you think. What is important to you. Everything else is just a tool.

The moment that my opportunity to rise in the ranks of the company came to a screeching halt, I spent a lot of time thinking about what my goals were. It was time to take a good look at my current career and life and decide what would come next.

During that introspective phase, one quote from a former HR director of the company bubbled up in my mind: "Success is not money or title. Success is doing what you want." At the time - 2 weeks into my post-college career - I thought she was delivering a corporate line to ensure that the 50 new joiners in the room would understand there can only be one CEO and we will most certainly not all make it to the top. So I discarded it. For 5 years, I fought that.

Then it dawned on me that this was one of the wisest statements anyone had ever uttered in my presence. When I took that to heart, in the following 5 years, I married the love of my life, traveled to the ends of the world and was even able to relocate across continents on the company's dime.

Will I ever be the CEO of that company? Highly unlikely. But that is also true if I had stuck to the path I was on. There's one CEO for tens of thousands of employees. There's one me for billions of people and I already occupy that body and mind. Why should I try for another role when I already have the one-in-10-billion role of a literal lifetime?

This is by far the most important strategy to success. Define what success means to you. Define what it means intrinsically, deep in your gut. What the world tells you does not matter. I started to focus on getting my personal life in order. I decided that moving across continents was more important than any promotion and I made it happen, on the company's dime. I decided I wanted to work from home and I made it happen (before COVID forced everyone).

The first and most important strategy to success:

- Set your own definition of success
- This definition will change over time, so take the time to reset at least once a year

4

Build Relationships

Think through how you got your current job. Think about how you met your significant other. Think about some of the best moments in your life. Odds are most of those happened thanks to somebody else. They may not have been your best friend or even a great acquaintance, but the reality is that life moves, changes and evolves with the people we encounter in it. This is true for the good and the bad.

In 2011, I was in college studying a scientific topic that has very little real world application. Most of the graduates simply went on to a PhD program. If you had reached that level, odds were you were book smart. In order to graduate, we all had to build a connection with at least one member of the academic staff. More often than not, that connection enabled an offer to transition into a PhD position after graduation. It was all so easy, and many chose that path.

Being uninterested, I talked about my options at a local sports club I was a member of. One of the other members was a highly successful executive at an insurance company. He suggested I go work for them for a few months and see if it's something I like. This random connection and simple conversation led to a 15 year career at three global companies, at ten jobs in five countries and two continents. That single connection started it all.

Originally, I had made no effort on building relationships with anyone outside of people I would consider friends. It all felt unnatural. My father had raised me to not use connections to get anything, not even an internship at his company. In hindsight that is probably one of the most damaging thoughts he ever shared with us. Everything runs on connections with other humans.

After that experience, I quickly learned that I should be strategic about building and keeping relationships with a wide variety of people.

As an introvert, it was necessary to get out of my comfort zone and reach out to colleagues. It was important to learn to connect with them and make sure they remembered who I was. I made it a point to identify something of value I could give them. Usually and especially at the beginning it was something small. A little help on their work. Insights on visiting a country I had been to. Whatever small favor that would help them. Soon, I had a vast network within the global company and I carefully nurtured it for over a decade. Despite colleagues moving in and out of the company, I'd accumulated connections on LinkedIn with about 5% of a 13,000 employee company. Considering that I was nowhere near being the CEO, that scale is massive. It takes years to build out.

But that effort was absolutely worth it. Whenever I got bored of my job, I knew someone in the team or near the job I was looking to get next. I never lacked at least one resource to get conversations going about my next role. Even when my role was threatened due to cut-backs, I knew I could reach out to dozens of colleagues who would try and retain me within the company. It was not a company made safety net. It was one I had intentionally built over the years. Moving from role to role, I made even more connections. More people got to see me at work and that expanded my network. People left the company so my network expanded beyond it and into countless countries.

The ultimate benefit from this decade-long work? When my wife decided she wanted to go back home, to a country where I did not have a visa, my network gave me the confidence that I could find the right job where the company would want to pay for my visa and all my expenses to relocate. It took a few months, but the deal stuck and I moved across continents on company dime. The cherry on top: because so many people at the company knew my work and me, I was able to relocate to a city where the company did not even have an office.

Strategy Two:

- Build your relationships intentionally
- It takes years so get started now

5

Connect People

The best outcome from strategy two is that you'll get to use strategy 3: create connections between people.

As anyone who's ever started a job at a large company knows, it is usually not clear who does what. From the evident - who's my HR contact if I have questions? - to the murkier - who is doing the account servicing for this region? - organizational charts are hard to come by and continuously evolve. Yet, the larger the organization, the more important it becomes to know who the relevant contact is before you step on their toes. Tasks and responsibilities are broken down to the lowest level possible and ambling around like an elephant will get you into trouble really quickly.

Having an affinity for organization and while applying strategy two, I quickly realized that I had a better understanding of who is who within my huge company than even some 20 year veterans. So I started paying attention to my colleagues' needs. They were looking for someone working on the tech we use, I would point them in the right direction. They needed someone working on the Latin American accounts? I would point them in the right direction. I quickly became a source of knowledge and value in our satellite office.

In your work life, half the battle is talking to the right person. If you find yourself repeating the same requests to a wide variety of people, it is because you have not found the right person or group of people. We all go through that. So if you are someone who can quickly pinpoint the relevant person and make an introduction for others, your value will grow exponentially.

Notice that it'll also compound with the previous strategy as creating value for new colleagues you meet becomes easier. Sometimes, it will be as easy as an intro email.

Moving to the world outside a company expands the value infinitely. I started off referring old college acquaintances for internships. This made the search so much less frustrating. Then you start referring job candidates. And finally, the most valuable of all: referring potential clients. Creating these warm introductions smooths out the process for everyone. Sometimes they are looking for someone and don't even know where to start. Sometimes a job ad yields only inadequate candidates. Sometimes you don't know where to find the product you are looking for. Those connections you make will not benefit you directly. In the short term, you'll gain nothing. But this is another effort that compounds greatly over time. The person whose first job was made possible by your efforts - trust me they'll remember you. If a day comes where they can pay you back, they will many times over. The knock on effect of receiving a little help from someone can be immense. And if you do it well and continuously, you'll have hundreds of people out there trying to pay you back when the time comes. Even if only a small fraction ever do, the value is incalculable.

Then there's the second level effect. Asking for a favor for yourself is one thing and usually people will do it, if it's reasonable. Asking for a favor for someone else is so much more powerful. Intrinsically people value selfless acts much more. Even if that same favor will cost them the same. The fact that you are asking for someone else will make it more likely that they will do it. Showing that you add value to others will reflect positively on everyone who sees it. They will remember you even if you did not help them directly. You will create a positive narrative about your person that yields dividends over years and decades.

Strategy Three:

- Always connect people with one another
- Do it selflessly and without expectations

6

Build Sales Skills

Sales gets a bad rap. It makes us uncomfortable. We picture the door-to-door salesman pushing his useless wares on the unsuspecting old lady. Just typing this up puts a pit in my stomach. Yet, sales make the world go round. There is nothing that is exchanged that is not in some form or shape a sale. If you spend time with a friend, they sold you on spending your precious limited resource that is time with them. They may have done it very naturally, such as by being nice, interested in what you say and offering appropriate advice.

Now re-read the previous sentence except replace friend with financial planner. They did not sell you on spending time with them. They are most likely trying to sell you on their services to improve your financial life. If we give the financial planner the benefit of the doubt and assume they have your best interest at heart, then the sales approach is no different to the friend who wants your time. In fact, I'd argue your money is less important than your time, so your friend's sell better be more honest.

The above may seem facetious, but the point remains: sales are everywhere and building your sales muscles is not optional in order to get the results you want. Imagine if you invented a car that had a 0% probability of crashing. You may be able to share those facts. But no one is going to invest in you and your idea if you can't sell them on it. Ultimately the act of selling is critical, lest your potential, your value and your ideas die a quiet death. Forget about the unethical salesmen. They are everywhere and they are not your concern. If no one sold, you would not buy many of the things you now cherish. In fact, the very machine I'm typing this on is a great example. I grew up in a windows/PC household. I disdained Apple and Macs. I thought they were for the weirdos. You couldn't even use excel on them. And yet over the years, Apple sold me on their design, on their products and on the experience of using their ecosystem. This would never have happened if they had not done the hard work of selling to me and a billion other people.

In the corporate world, even if you are not in an explicit sales role, selling is fundamental. First and foremost, you need to sell your work. If you create a model and you improve something on what was done before, you need to sell it. You need to sell it so the person whose work you improved is not insulted but rather grateful for you. Do it wrong and they will assume you are trying to show them up. Do it wrong and your work, although objectively better, will be rejected and they will label you a failure.

When you are introducing yourself to a new colleague, sell yourself. Why should they want to work with you? What makes you unique and particularly skilled in that position? It is natural for us all to not want to work with the cook when we need a tech product. If we want delicious food, we'll go the other way around. And we want to know that the cook is not a fast food burger flipper, although sometimes we do!

When you are applying the strategies elaborated earlier in this book, you have to sell too. You have to sell yourself to justify why someone should keep in touch with you. You have to sell the people you are introducing to one another and why there is value in that. All those acts represent a small sale.

And of course no company makes any money without sales. So whether you are a natural salesperson or a numbers guy and introvert like myself, build sales skills.

After my first year and a half, it was time to change jobs. My full-time position was being eliminated and I knew that 6 months in advance. Being at the beginning of my career, I knew that this represented an opportunity. I could leave with no hard feelings. I also knew I wanted to go to a different office in a different country. I used my network to get a few options and was in fact offered three wildly different positions in 2 different countries. One represented adventure from a location perspective, but the role was focused on financial analysis. It was in fact fully in my comfort zone. Although I would have learned more about financial analysis, I also would have stagnated in many other ways. A second role was a lateral move to a different less exciting country and one hundred percent in a comfort role. The third option which I did not chase originally represented a drastic change. I would be moving to a boring country. The role itself did not require my number crunching skills and I in fact thought of that group of colleagues as less than. But it then dawned on me that I would be the most technical person in that team and learn how to sell. They were fundamentally a sales team. I ended up spending four years in that team learning everything I could about sales. I was so successful despite being outside my comfort zone that I got the best bonuses of my career, beating many of my more experienced colleagues over multiple years. It opened the entire company up to my whims. I was primed to succeed. That was before my manager was then forcibly removed and any chance of promotion within that team disappeared. But I had acquired something more valuable than that promotion. With my sales skills and my good reputation, I was now able to get any role I wanted at the company. And

I went to a team where I would have no place if all they did was look at my resume. I sold them on why they should bring me on board. I opened up a whole new realm of possibilities.

Strategy Four:

- Get out of your comfort zone and build sales skills
- Ideally take on a sales role

7

Work For Your Manager

While it may seem obvious, your manager is the single most important person at any job you have. You need to learn to manage your manager. There are an infinite number of ways that a manager can help or hinder you in your career. Understanding your manager and their goals is as important as breathing in and out. If you fail to do so, you will either stagnate and wither, or even be pushed out.

In my second job, where I was learning how to sell, my manager let me get away with anything. I still got promotions and wonderful bonuses. How did I achieve that? I worked hard to understand him and in particular what would make him look great to his own boss. This is no secret, but I see hundreds of colleagues doing it wrong every year. The most important work you can do in a job is to make your boss look like a genius. Making yourself shine will get you into trouble more often than not.

My manager was an older guy, getting close to retirement. His priority was clearly to remain comfortable and survive until retirement. He had no ambitions to climb any higher and was largely happy where he was.

He got to travel a lot and did not have to put in much work. However he had large blind spots. He was not a technology guy. He was also not very technical. He did not pay attention to detail. There were all things I excelled at. Over the course of the following three years, I made sure that our team was at the forefront of any tech initiatives the company threw at us. We looked like the tech transformation champions for the whole department. I made sure that our technical expertise increased. I took it upon myself to review any work that was referred beyond our team and needed to be looked at by the technical center of expertise. Why me despite my youth and inexperience? Although I needed to refer to the older team member's expertise, I had a detailed way of communicating and structuring documents that got us almost any deal approved. I even went so far as to challenge the technical set-up of our pricing. I was able to leverage the experience from the team and my attention to detail into more referrals and more approvals. My manager looked like a genius. The team had been turned around. We were making more big deals than all other teams in the department combined.

I also noticed that his manager had a metric which required all his teams to self-identify when something had gone wrong. Upper management knew that with a group of about 100 people all selling across the continent, things fell through the cracks. Things were approved that should not have been. They knew there was a minimum error rate and they wanted to self-identify before an audit team came around. This was a challenge for most individuals as you never want to raise your hand and tell your boss and his boss that you messed up. I figured out that that was actually a positive thing, assuming the mess-up did not have a significant financial impact. In fact, the department head needed to have a minimum rate of self identified issues every year to get his highest possible bonus. So I made it a point to identify errors and raise them to their awareness. These mistakes had to be significant enough that they had to be reported, but ideally not so significant that the company would lose millions of dollars. As it turns out, this was merely a matter of patience. The team churned out errors all the time. Mostly they were not even worth mentioning, but the odd one would be and I'd immediately file an incident report.

So not only had I made my direct manager look good, but I was helping his manager optimize his bonus. I cannot tell you how much that was worth to me, both in actual monetary terms, but also in terms of opportunity later in my career. I would always have this executive promoting me and helping me out.

Now it is important to note that some managers misunderstand your intentions. In some of the following jobs I had, it was a little harder to understand my managers. The biggest challenge is when they are a micromanager. Because at that point they constantly talk about your work. They want to correct details and watch over your shoulder. It becomes even difficult to know what their bigger picture goals are. Watch out for micromanagers. It is impossible to satisfy them and fulfill their goals. They obviously have their priorities wrong and it is very hard to change that for them. At that point, after giving it enough effort, it is often worth cutting your losses and moving on. I had to do that twice in my career. Unfortunately, for some the Peter Principle does not motivate them to grow. It just caps their capabilities. The Peter Principle states that you will be promoted until you reach your level of incompetence. I take that as a challenge to become more competent. Others take it as an invitation to desperately cling to that position.

Strategy Five:

- Win for your manager
- Don't make yourself shine, make your boss shine

8

Focus on ONE Thing

Distraction, attention, mind-share. We live in a world obsessed with attention. Social media and digital media in general have created a world where everyone is competing for our attention. We all have 24 hours in a day and the struggle is very real.

At work, we all start with one responsibility on the first day. Because we are new and eager to prove ourselves, we take on more. We say yes to the boss' side project. We create our own side project because we have a knack for technology that no one else in the team has. Before we realize it, our to-do list has grown beyond control. And that does not even include the inbox, the bane of the office worker's life. That gets out of hand at an exponentially faster rate.

There are so many books out there to help manage your time or prioritize better. Time is not managed. Time simply is. It keeps flowing and there's nothing you can do about it. You have 24 hours in a day and if you exclude the very necessary time for sleeping, eating and other basic human functions, it is gone before you even know what happened.

The next myth is that you have to be able to multitask. Multi-tasking is not real. Not even computers multitask effectively. When you switch from one activity to another, you effectively stop one and start another. Switching back incurs the same cost. That is real for computers. That is even more real for us humans. Ever noticed that you can walk and talk? What if the topic changes to a complex math problem? You stop walking. That's because the mental friction to do one then the other and back to the first makes it pointless to do both. Now this compounds with mental tasks at work. We are constantly monitoring the email inbox, while trying to actually complete our work or attending a meeting. Meetings themselves are for the most part unfocused without a clear purpose or agenda. The only thing that is clear about a meeting is that it will last as long as the time you scheduled it for, if not longer. They are only rarely shorter.

My trick to cut through all the noise is to pick the ONE thing. What is that one action, project, client that you need to work on today to make the day successful. Sometimes, it's cleaning out your inbox. Sometimes, it's answering a single email. That email will have a trickle down effect on all your other work. Now this may seem obvious in certain circumstances. The one big client that represents 80% of your portfolio? Of course you drop everything to attend to them. But what if it's more subtle? You have 20 or 50 clients of about the same size. They all need your attention throughout the day. How do you address that?

This is where taking that step back becomes more important than even in the obvious cases. Those 50 clients all needing something from you at the same time points to a systemic problem. You should either not have 50 clients, or you should be servicing them in a better way. No one can expect you to answer 50 client demands on a daily basis.

At one point I was dealing with 200 clients, none of which were simple. They were not incredibly complex, but rarely would I get an email relating to one of them that could be answered within 5-10 minutes.

However, when I took a step back, it also became clear that some of those requests were not urgent. Many were not, in fact. Often I could let the email sit until someone either called me or the problem went away. Soon I started to understand which emails needed immediate attention and which could be solved by waiting or letting someone else answer. I removed myself from the process wherever possible.

The next step was to then focus purely on high impact actions, with clients and internally too. If it would help solve a problem for multiple people, it likely was worth attention. If not, those people would figure it out. I started removing myself from meetings. When you start your career, you feel proud to be included in meetings. Eventually many learn that it's best not to be included. Some never learn and are even insulted if you left them off a meeting where they would not have been able to contribute meaningfully. But you should realize that attending those meetings will prevent you from completing work that will have an actual impact. Something that will move you to the next level.

A simple trick to figure out what is truly important: stop answering emails while you are out of office. When you are back, see who follows up. Those are the important ones.

The same is true in your social life. If you say yes to every invitation that comes your way, you will end up an alcoholic that is stretched for time. There is so much abundance in the world and a single person will never see it all, live it all. Accept that fact and focus on the few events that mean something to you.

I use this same strategy for travel. The internet will have us believe that you need to visit as many places as possible and do as many things as possible every trip. So what if you've been to every major European city? So what if you went to Paris for two days on a five-stop seven-day trip that included the Eiffel Tower, the Louvre and the Palace in Versailles. Do you think you actually experienced Paris? Did you get a true experience out of those two days? Slow down and make it a seven-day trip in Paris. Take the time to walk around and see where the locals go. Browse a random grocery store. That single experience will stay longer with you than anything you saw up on the Eiffel Tower.

Getting back to work: focus on the one project, the one client, the one activity that will move the needle for you. Give it your best and ignore the rest.

Strategy Six:

- Slow down and focus on the ONE thing
- Everything else is noise

9

Learn to Delegate

I can already hear your brain: but I'm an individual contributor. I have no team to delegate to.

You are right, you don't have a team to assign tasks to. The reality is that most managers are bad at delegating. They are great at assigning tasks. And sometimes not even that. True delegation is when the thought process and decision making process is taken out of your hands. At that point, you become either a sounding board or someone who is sought out for higher level decisions.

Delegating can happen in all directions. You don't just delegate down. You can delegate to a peer or to a manager. The truth is that some decisions should not be in your hands. And you need to make sure you put them in the right hands. Delegation also includes automation. We all have a limited decision making ability every day. At the end of a day full of decisions, I feel drained. I can't even decide what to eat for dinner. Especially with a buffet of options available at my fingertips via our smartphones.

Some people take delegation to the extremes and wear the same thing every day. That effectively completely removes the decision making process. It sounds absurd but it works magic. Building habits essentially delegates tasks to lower level cognitive functions, reserving your time and energy to other, more important thoughts. I've delegated my morning routine to automation. I know when I get up, when I feed my cats, when I make coffee, when I start working. This all happens so automatically that on the rare occasion where I am sick, or hungover, I STILL do those things. I only start feeling bad after I've completed the automation process. Once I settled into a fresh task, that's when it hits me that I am not 100%.

One of my bosses was once called by a client who was upset about a decision I made. My manager simply told the client that he should talk to me and see if I was willing to change my mind. That's true delegation right there. My manager did not take it upon himself to challenge me in front of the client. He trusted my decision making process. He knew that if it was an issue, I would have come to him for guidance.

In fact, when a decision is clearly too big for me, instead of working on it for ages, trying to make sure I do it right, I put together my thoughts, giving options and clearly stating my preference. Then I delegate it back to my manager. This is a simple trick that will cut down on days and days of anguish. Your manager will be pleased. You did not just throw your hands up and give up. You also did not move forward recklessly. However, you did place the responsibility back on them, as it should be. Doing this skillfully will save countless hours of worry and anxiety.

Along those same lines, I would encourage to delegate to peers whenever possible. You may think this will make you seem lazy or like you are not pulling your weight. In fact, this simply highlights your awareness of how much you can tackle at any point in time. Having a peer do it is much much better than having no one do it. My favorite trick is to skip meetings where many of my peers are attending too. This means they can take on the tasks and follow-ups. If it's too much to handle or something impacts me specifically, they will let me know. You do have to keep your ego in check for this one though. It may make you feel excluded or like you are less than. In fact your time is more important than being a shadow for your peers.

Strategy Seven:

- Delegate front, center and back.
- Always ensure you are the right person to be addressing a problem. If not, pass it along.

10

Say Yes (When Relevant)

Now this one contradicts strategy 6. But only a little. And in case you didn't know, humans are full of contradictions, so if anything I am showing you that A.I. did not write this book!

While focusing on one thing is key, you also want to understand what that one thing could be one year from now, or 5 years from now. Say you are a bank teller and your goal is to become an AI engineer. Focusing on the ONE thing that makes you successful at the bank will not lead you to your goal of being an AI engineer. You are going to have to take on more.

Early in my career, I was wrongly advised to always say yes when approached for an extra set of hands on company projects. Before I knew it, I was in 5-6 projects, dedicating an ever decreasing amount of time to each and not really achieving results in any. I was stressed and stretched. Every project was a side-project and a hobby. And the biggest problem was that everyone operated in the same way. It was a cultural sickness in the organization. We all were constantly encouraged to have too much on our plates with the end result that nothing ever got done.

After purging myself of most hobbies after a job change, I knew I did not want to end up in the same spot, so I said no to almost everything. I was very picky about where I involved myself. This was a year and half into my career. I was not senior enough to say no, but I was human enough to say: I don't think I can dedicate the time you need me to in order to be effective and help you drive this forward. It works. No one wants dead weight on their projects. And yet that's all they ever recruited. Did I mention contradictions?

That being said, I took on a project to help modernize our technology. I gave it a significant share of my time and attention. I took it so seriously that I vetoed the launch at the last minute and that action was escalated up to the COO. At just shy of 3 years into my career, I was sat in front of the COO to explain why I was putting my veto on the COO's pet project. I thought I would be let go then and there. There was precedent. Get onboard with the tech transformation or move on.

Lucky for me, I had dedicated time to understanding the challenges we were facing and why our community would simply not use the new software. There were some evident flaws that only someone in my position could see. I explained this in great detail to the COO and he agreed with me. The launch was delayed by 6 months to be able to address the flaws. To be honest, they were not all addressed and we still launched an inadequate system six months later, but nonetheless, progress had been made and I could stand in front of my colleagues to share what I honestly thought and help them adapt.

At the time, I thought I had picked the first (side-)project to drop on my lap and went all in. What I did not realize is that the same project would uncover opportunities for me years and decades later. I had a real passion for technology in the service of the business. Although not part of my job description and if I had not done it, no one would have blinked an eye, joining that project opened doors years down the line that I could not anticipate then. I currently enjoy a leadership role under the Chief Data Officer of my company. Before that project, I had zero knowledge of tech or data. It took some building up, but it coalesced into an executive role just 10 years later.

These days I am much more intentional about this. I even explicitly help provide opportunities like this to younger colleagues.

If you have a job in an area that is not the vertical you want to grow into, find a way to lend your time to an area where you will grow into your next job, or the one after that. Never lose sight of your future and start building those skills now. A leader I admired once took it to a further level and told me: apply only for jobs that will give you the next job you want. The message is clear. Focus on the skills you acquire and stretch yourself only where it aligns with your goals and ambition.

Strategy Eight:

- Find ways to grow your skills by joining the right projects
- Be extra picky and intentional

11

Take Responsibility

This is probably the most underrated of these strategies. Once I was made aware of it, I could not stop seeing people make this mistake everywhere. Humans are defensive. We want to justify our actions. We never intend any harm. We want to be perfect. The only problem is that we are not and we tend to make it worse by deflecting responsibility.

It is natural, especially in a work setting to not bring attention to yourself in a negative way. Say you are the last one out of the office and forgot to lock up. Is it your fault? Building security should have checked and protected the building from intruders. Those intruders should not have been there in the first place. You got unlucky. The other guy left the office open over three days last year and nothing happened. There are unlimited ways to shift the responsibility. The reality is that something going wrong is almost always a confluence of different events with different responsible parties. Own your part.

Humans are error prone. We make mistakes all day every day. Whenever I am driving, I pay attention. Everyone is terrible at driving. Except for me of course. No! This is precisely the wrong thought process. I am the worst driver out there and I need to protect others from me. Do you see how that shift in mindset keeps both you and others safer on the roads? Imagine if everyone changed their perspective to that. How many people do you think would cut you off (intentionally)? How many people would be speeding?

I will admit that this is a hard one to implement. I grew up as the middle child, sandwiched between the golden boy and the baby of the family. Unfortunately for me, I also function at a million miles an hour and was constantly butting heads with my siblings. This created a lot of conflict and by default, as the troublemaker, I was at fault. I was blamed countless times for incidents that were not of my doing. As such, I grew conditioned to deflect blame. It did not matter if someone was accusing me of anything or simply asking a clarifying question. "It's not my fault" was my default reaction. It still is sometimes, and I catch it after the fact. It's deep programming for me and many others. But it is destructive. Highly destructive.

When I first met my wife, she would ask me where I was, if I was not home by 6 or 7 pm. In my mind it was none of her business and why is she even asking? What is she accusing me of? The sad part is that I was either at work or at the gym 99% of those times. Eventually it got to the point where I started going to bars and have a drink. Since I was being accused of wrongdoing, why not actually do something wrong? I don't need to finish that story to make my point. Defensiveness and poor communication skills led us down a nasty path before we recovered. And one part of that was learning to take responsibility. I may not have intentionally done anything wrong, but even poor communication or a forgotten heads-up could be misinterpreted. And that was all on me.

The very same principle applies at work. Corporations are huge machines that are exchanging millions of emails a year. People are on the phones, in meetings, texting and communicating in every other way but smoke signals. This leads inevitably to breakdowns all over the place. And odds are you are at least partially responsible more often than you admit even to yourself. From the classic email sent without an attachment to a colleague left of the cc line, the small errors compound. We all do them. Sometimes the mistakes or missed targets are larger. Or we make commitments we can't possibly uphold. In those moments, there is only one thing to do: take responsibility. It does not matter if it was 100% your fault or 1% your fault, taking responsibility for the entire issue is critical.

Although in the short term, it may not be a great experience, over time your colleagues and friends will learn that they can trust you. You are not the perfect one. You are the one that shares when something has gone wrong. At worst, they are aware earlier than if they have to investigate. At best, they catch issues before they snowball into real problems.

The trust you build along the way is invaluable.

Strategy Nine:

- Take responsibility when things don't go as planned
- Even if it's a combination of factors, own it, learn from it and move on

12

Always Keep Growing

When I was in school, I thought learning was easy. You just listen to the teachers, you solve the problems and you're done. I have a mind that retains facts astonishingly well. I never had to sit down and truly study for anything until college. My education was diversified across biology, history, mathematics, literature, languages and a bunch of other things. I liked essentially all subjects. I was also good at everything in school, so that made it easier.

When I got to college, I was focused on math and physics. My world narrowed and I felt constrained. It felt like I was being limited in my learning. I could not really identify why it did not feel good, but I knew I had to do something. So, despite majoring in physics, with a tough course load at one of the best physics programs in the world, I took on additional courses in things like philosophy of mathematics, chemistry or Japanese. I added completely random additional courses to feel like I was getting a well rounded education. I thought my education would be coming to an end soon and I wanted to make sure I had as many tools in my belt as possible. My father always preached: keep as many doors open as possible. You never know which one you might need.

The problem with that mindset is that you never truly commit. Imagine being a roofer carrying every type of tool up on the roof, when they truly only need a hammer and a nail gun. It makes their job impossible. And that's exactly the big issue I had at that point.

I then joined the workforce and started learning real world applications of the theoretical stuff from college. Once again the world became narrow, but also it did not. You see, when you apply statistics to insurance, you are not only discussing numbers. Those numbers represent fires, floods, earthquakes and so many other things. Those numbers need to be explained to a manager or a client. Those numbers are imperfect and you can easily argue up or down. The narrative becomes important. And your peers may have a different opinion, so you have to sell them on it. Or you have to present your thoughts and ideas in front of 10, 50 or 1000 people.

My growth curve accelerated and I was blown away by how little I knew. I had always seen myself as a highly educated person and suddenly I was a naive ignorant newbie. We all go through that as we join the workforce.

As you settle into all of that, your growth curve flattens and you start feeling comfortable in many areas. You no longer worry about speaking up in a meeting if you disagree. You no longer get anxious that the email you sent may have a misspelling here or there. You come up with systems to ensure you minimize your errors and omissions. Work becomes a routine. Many get comfortable and spend a lifetime in a job they never truly cared for from the start. But they know how to do it and it pays the bills. You live for the weekend, for the vacation (if you can afford it).

That routine terrified me. I could see my colleagues who had been doing this for 10 or 20 years and I knew only one thing: I don't want to be them in 10 years, or even in 5. So what's the solution?

Keep growing. Find a way to make yourself uncomfortable. Open your mind to the possibilities and make sure you pick a new path regularly. Or take the next bend to see what's behind it. Use strategy 8 to help you do this intentionally.

In your spare time, read business books, memoirs, even self-help books. Listen to podcasts or courses, or whatever works for you. Don't worry about finding THE right information. The goal is to hear a multitude of perspectives and ideas. Expand your mind, evaluate other's thoughts, processes and systems. Take what you like and what works for you and leave the rest behind. This book itself is a great example. These are all great strategies, but you can't simply use them the exact same way I did. You will need to modify and adapt. Learn what works for you. How it works for you.

One particular aspect of growth that is important to address very intentionally: your weaknesses. If you read the chapter on my path to sales, you'll have noticed I intentionally addressed a gap in my skill set. I proactively stretched myself into a new job that would help me learn the skills in a quintessential area. I am not a prototypical salesperson. I never wanted a career in sales, but I knew that my future success would depend on me learning a minimum set of skills in sales.

Similarly, identify your gaps and weaknesses. Ask peers and managers to help you with this as self-awareness is not always 20:20. Prioritize the list and start working on it. It is important to rely on your strengths for success, but equally it is important to raise the standard of your weakest critical skills. They say a team is as strong as its weakest link. Your skills are a team. All your skills put together make up who you are as a professional. Strengthening the weakest link in your inner skills team will help you grow and be successful.

If you keep working at your growth, in life and at work, you will see the results. They will not be immediate, but the compounding effects will lead to greatness.

Strategy Ten:

- Always be growing
- Be intentional with direction and commitment to it
- Address your weaknesses

13

Do The Work

All of the strategies shared so far are nuggets. They remind me of the mushroom you pick up in Super Mario. You get taller and acquire new skills to increase your chances of success. But the mushroom alone will not do it. You still need to move forward and jump when needed. You still need to do the work.

As shared earlier, it was always easy for me to perform at school. Until I went to college, I had no idea what it was like to work for anything. Even in college, I went through the motions and succeeded with minimum effort for the most part. I thought I was lucky. It did make the first 20 odd years of my life easy. It also made the next stage a little harder. I had never learned to work for something. When you join the workforce, very little is done for you. If you don't put in the work, no one will do it for you.

And the work you do has to be of high quality. While hard work alone will get you nowhere, it is a combination of high quality work and the other strategies that will unlock and unleash your potential.

If you perform high quality work for someone, then they become part of your network and will advocate for you. They will also have more faith in the connections you make for them. All those introductions are only valuable if they know that the quality of your work is high. Then the quality of your connections is also assumed to be high.

Selling is easier when you have a high quality product or service. You can deliver on your manager's goal only if you know how to complete it in a way that matches or exceeds their own standards. You can afford to focus only on the most important thing if you provide high quality. If you neglect other parts of your work, you need to be able to point to the one thing you did do and how that value was bigger than anything else you could have worked on. Exceeding expectations on the quality of your work will allow you to pass tasks and projects to others as you can justify your value elsewhere if those things are taken care of. On the flip side, if you want to be a part of a project outside of your core job description, you need to show that having you onboard will be a benefit to the team.

Whatever field you work in, there is a minimum standard of the output you share. Make sure you surpass that, so you can leverage the other strategies to the fullest.

Strategy Eleven:

- Do high quality work

14

Slow Down

The modern world would have us believe that we have no time. The day has 24 hours, but you are expected to sleep for 8, work for 8 and somehow do everything else in 8. The devices that make so many things accessible, also mean we are constantly connected, constantly aware of what is happening outside our lives. We feel this need to keep up with it. With work, we constantly get emails. In theory, you could easily work 16 hours a day every day. The problem is that the more work you get done, the more work will be sent your way. There is no catching up. There is no "done". In large corporations, there is always more work to be done.

In life as in work, the only option is to slow down. Do the work, do it right, but do it at a pace that keeps you sane and productive. If you just deliver on your to-do list over and over, you will burn out. And quality will suffer. This goes back to the previous strategy. You cannot deliver quality work if you are constantly rushing through.

When you are in the gym, you need to slow your movements. Make the exercise clean and correct. That will help you improve. The same is true at work. Do your projects right. Spend time reviewing and practicing your presentation. It is so important to spend the right amount of time and dedicate the proper effort.

Strategy Twelve:

- Take the necessary time to deliver quality work
- More work is always around the corner. Don't fall for it.

15

Bringing It All Together

J ust like there are millions of ways to live a life, there are millions of ways to be successful at work. These 12 strategies represent archetypes that can accelerate the path to success. These will only work if you are self-aware and apply them conscientiously. It is critical to embed them in your mind, in your work, in your routine. A one-off use of any of these will not yield the results you are looking for. All these strategies combine and compound by themselves and together. The power comes together over time. Given enough effort and time, it will surprise you how things just seem to magically come together.

Stay vigilant and come back to this book or another one. We all gravitate back to what's easy, what's comfortable. You work on these strategies and achieve a result. Then you find the next iteration that will help you get to the next. There is no limit to what you can achieve, based on these archetypes. The only limitation is to fall back into a comfort zone.

In parting, I'd like to leave you with a warning. Do not compare yourself to others. Success is all about you, your thoughts, your actions. Others will succeed too. Be happy for them. Do not let negative thoughts in. Do not compare! Life is full of unknowns. It is not transparent. They may work hard on one thing and succeed. You may only see their actions as it relates to you and that may be something they choose not to spend time on. They may have a lucky streak and be at the right place at the right time. They may have made the right connection years ago and it finally pays dividends even though they were struggling recently. That is something to be celebrated. In their shoes, you'd breathe a sigh of relief and embrace the success as you've been working on it for years.

Be thankful when success comes your way. All sorts of external factors could slow you down or make you move faster than you are comfortable with. Always make sure to embrace it and move forward. Review your goals regularly and make sure you are still working towards what matters most to you.

I hope all these strategies will help you take your career and your life to the next level, and I look forward to the day someone references back to this book and writes a better one that encapsulates everything I've shared and more.